Walter Farley's
How to Stay Out of
Trouble with Your Horse

Walter Farley's
How to Stay Out of Trouble with Your Horse

Some Basic Safety Rules
to Help You Enjoy Riding

by the author of
THE BLACK STALLION Books

with photographs by Tim Farley

DOUBLEDAY & COMPANY, INC.
GARDEN CITY, NEW YORK

To the memory of
Captain William Heyer,
world-renowned *Haute École* rider,
whose horses wanted to please him.

Library of Congress Cataloging in Publication Data

Farley, Walter, 1915–
    Walter Farley's How to stay out of trouble with
your horse.
    Includes index.
    SUMMARY: Enumerates ways to avoid the accidents
and serious injuries that may occur when working
with horses.
    1. Horsemanship—Safety measures—Juvenile
literature. [1. Horsemanship—Safety measures.
2. Safety] I. Farley, Tim. II. Title.
III. Title: How to stay out of trouble with your
horse.
SF309.2.F37   798.2'3'0289
    ISBN: 0-385-15480-1 Trade
    ISBN: 0-385-15481-x Prebound
    Library of Congress Catalog Card Number 79–8922

Acknowledgments

I would like to express my thanks and gratitude to the professional horse people who assisted me in putting this book together: to Stanley White and Buck Grass, well-known trainers of Arabian show horses; to Chaille Groom, artist, trainer, and show rider for Brusally Ranches in Scottsdale, Arizona, where most of the photographs were taken; to Paula Turner, who taught Seattle Slew, the undefeated Triple Crown Winner, his first lessons; to Angie Draper, who raises horses as well as paints portraits of the most famous race horses in the United States; and to all my friends of the Y-Knot 4-H Saddle Club, in Portage County, Ohio, and its Safety Committee, who know that horse safety makes horse sense.

W.F.

Contents

The external anatomy of a horse. Drawing by Chaille Groom.

Introduction—
A Letter to Young Riders

Dear Horse People,

For forty years now I have been writing books about tall, fiery stallions and a boy who loved them and was able to control them. The stories are known as *The Black Stallion* and *The Island Stallion* books. The first story was a childhood fantasy for I had no horse, only a dream—that of a great black stallion who loved me as I loved him. I put the dream down on paper as a youngster and it became a book, which led to other books in *The Black Stallion* series and enabled me to raise and enjoy horses of my own.

After a lifetime of writing horse books and, most important, observing and working with professional horse people in every facet of the sport, I was taken back not long ago to that beginning dream.

We were on the island of Sardinia in the Mediterranean making *The Black Stallion* movie, based on my first book. As I watched the boy, Alec, and The Black come together on that remote island, I realized that what I believed as a child, I believe now.

It is possible—in fact, necessary—to regard your horse not as a working machine whose only true love is the feed you give him but as a close friend and to love him. In fact, the professional horse people who may "put down" love and honest sentiment between horse and rider usually are without feelings and sensitivity themselves. It has been proven countless times on the racetrack, show-ring, and barnyard. Call it what you like—love, friendship, compatibility—but there is a *union* between horse and rider that is understood by each.

This union, however, works between rider and mount only when combined with the rider's hard work, patience, perseverance, kindness, tact, and, of course, experience, however you get it. And if you truly care for your horse and develop an understanding with him, you will not only have a friend but will acquire greater courage, confidence, and awareness of yourself.

Be that as it may for you, it is a serious responsibility to own a horse. It is *you* who will make him what he is to become—a healthy, well-conditioned, well-mannered, and safe animal, a joy and pride to ride, or a pampered pet who is spoiled and unsafe for you to own and ride. If you achieve the former, that is really loving your horse. If the latter, heaven help you.

The purpose of this short book is not to help you train your horse but to help you avoid the accidents and serious injuries that befall many of us who work with horses, especially those who are starting out, though by no means restricted to them. As it is in driving a car, motorcycle, or anything else, mistakes will be made by an amateur and a professional alike, but very often it is the simple things overlooked through carelessness which cause the most problems and accidents.

For example, I have seen a professional horseman hurt seriously simply by not using a halter lead line when he went to get his favorite, aged horse in pasture. When he took hold of the horse's halter, he unthinkingly slipped two of his fingers into the halter ring.

The horse shied at something on the way back to the barn and his handler could not get his fingers loose from the ring. The horse panicked and dragged the man the length of the field. A very simple mistake caused the accident.

It is with this in mind that I have set down some basic safety rules, few in number and as concise as I can make them, all in the hope that you will read, reread, and try to remember them.

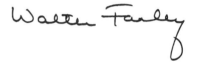

Walter Farley's
How to Stay Out of
Trouble with Your Horse

Be sure that you have had qualified, competent instruction in riding before you buy your own horse.

1
Buying Your Horse

Probably the most common reason for horse accidents among young riders is the lack of competent guidance and help. In no other sport are young people so improperly supervised as in the selection, riding, and care of horses. And yet in each horse we are dealing with about a thousand pounds of strength and energy in a very sensitive animal!

Often, parents have asked me as to the kind and type of horse they should purchase for their children, most of whom have had little or no experience with horses. Uppermost in the parents' mind is that they want a *safe* horse. My advice has always been the same: "Spend your money on qualified, competent instruction before buying a horse for your child."

There are very few areas in the United

States where the basic fundamentals in the care and riding of horses cannot be learned. It might be an equitation school, a riding academy, or, if neither, instruction gained through the acquaintance or knowledge of a horse person who is willing and able to teach the basics of good horsemanship. Also, there are 4-H clubs, pony clubs, and saddle clubs in most every area where there are horses. A young person should join one of them, attend the meetings, and study their manuals on horse care—all before accepting the heavy responsibility of owning his or her horse.

However, regardless of how strongly I feel about this, I can recall only a few ever taking this advice. To disappoint their children by not buying them a horse is more than they can bear, especially since their children "love horses so very much and want one of their own."

If this is the case, I want to warn you, the young owner, that you can take a beautiful horse home only to find out he's a hopeless, useless idiot. To avoid this, I suggest you do two things. First, have an experienced horse person assist you in making your selection. If possible get a professional to help you buy, one who has *your* interest at heart and not that of the dollars in his pocket, one who is not selling the horse or collecting a commission from the seller. It will save you money, time, and concern if such a person is found before purchasing your horse.

My second suggestion is that you have a veterinarian check out the horse's health and soundness. And, if possible, arrange to have a week's trial of the horse to find out if he's right for you. If that isn't possible, the least the seller can do is mount the horse and ride him for you. See for yourself how well he is trained and what he can do with the seller in the saddle. A safe bet is that the horse will perform about one half as well for you.

There are other things you should keep in mind as you select this "horse of your own." Remember he will make or break you, as you will him.

* * *

1. A good disposition in a horse is as

important as good conformation. You want to be friends, not do battle!

2. Don't "overhorse" yourself. A high-strung horse requires an experienced rider. Buy a horse that suits your ability at this time, not one you hope to be able to control and ride at a later date. If you want a good all-around horse, don't buy a "specialty" horse. Buy what you need *now*.

3. Stallions, in most cases, should be purchased only by breeding farms and professionals. I realize this seems near heresy after all the books I've written on the close relationship between Alec Ramsay and the Black Stallion, as well as Steve Duncan and Flame, the Island Stallion. But Alec and Steve had no choice and they lived under unusual circumstances in stories of adventure.

I'm not saying that you would not, in time, be able to handle and control a stallion, only that in most cases it will be more work than fun. As it is with any animal, much depends on the temperament of the stallion. I have seen and owned some as docile and tractable as any gelding. I know many horse people who will have nothing but stallions in their barns. However, more often than not, stallions are far more of a handful and a responsibility than mares or geldings, especially if you are stabled in a mixed barn and want to ride in mixed company. My suggestion is that you wait a while before purchasing a stallion who will challenge your ability to the utmost. Wait until you feel you are ready to cope with him and whatever problems may come up. There is time enough for that, and you and your horse will be better for it.

4. Mares are sometimes moody and unpredictable, especially when they're "in season." But if you understand her moods, a mare can be your favorite (this is so for me, even though I have stallions and write about them). If you plan to pasture your mare with others, be observant as to how she gets along with them. Often one mare tends to be "boss" and goes about it in earnest.

5. Geldings are a very pleasant and serviceable type of horse. Some people say, "You can't beat a good gelding for all-around usefulness and as a friend." They are far less trouble than stallions or mares in most respects and their attitudes, temperaments, and dispositions are the same every day; good or bad as they may be, they will change very little, it at all. Don't underestimate the courage and ability of geldings when comparing them to stallions, for some of the greatest American racehorses have been geldings—Kelso and Forego, as examples.

2
Grooming Your Horse

Now that you have your horse at home, the work as well as the fun begins. Remember that I have said in the Introduction that the rider's love for a horse is not enough without his or her patience, kindness, perseverance, and work. And what experience you need will come as you get to know your horse and learn what he and you can and cannot do. Meanwhile, let's not make any mistakes we cannot rectify and which might cause injury to your horse or yourself. Keep in mind that your horse is amazingly intuitive. He is not the "dumb beast" many people (even horse people) would have you believe. His friendship cannot be won only through his stomach. He can sense your personality and mood. Feelings of fear, hostility, or a genuine liking for him are instantly felt by your horse.

The best thing I know for you to do with a new horse in the stable is to *watch* him. In general, try to detect his feelings and moods, to understand him as much as possible. Each horse has his own unique character. Watch him at liberty and in the barn. Then in the days to come you can respond to what you have learned about him. If he is frightened, you will try to calm him. If he is bored, you will try to inspire him. If he is restless, you will try to be patient. If he is rebellious, you will try to be firm.

All these things you need to do are very special, of course, horse person or not. If your horse helps you develop these qualities of patience and understanding, he will not only have a place in your stable but in your life as well.

None of these training abilities will be acquired overnight. You are dealing with a very special and particularly sensitive animal, not a machine. Your task is to develop an extremely subtle communication between yourself and your horse, so you will understand each other and have trust and respect for each other. Don't underestimate the power of your voice in communicating with him. He will learn that the *sound* of your words mean different things to him, not only commands to "walk," "trot," and "canter" but also "You are my friend and I want to get along with you." Many of us carry on long conversations with our horses, even to the point of telling them our personal problems. Try it. You may find that it helps you as much as it does your horse. One way or the other, it is very worthwhile communication.

Daily grooming is your first chore in conditioning your horse and getting to know every inch of him. It can be rough and dangerous at times, and there are rules to follow. Some are very simple. Some you know. But all bear repeating and remembering.

* * *

1. *Do not smoke in the stable area.* A fire is hell. And for the same reason, don't block exits with equipment. In case of emergency, you and your horse need to get out.

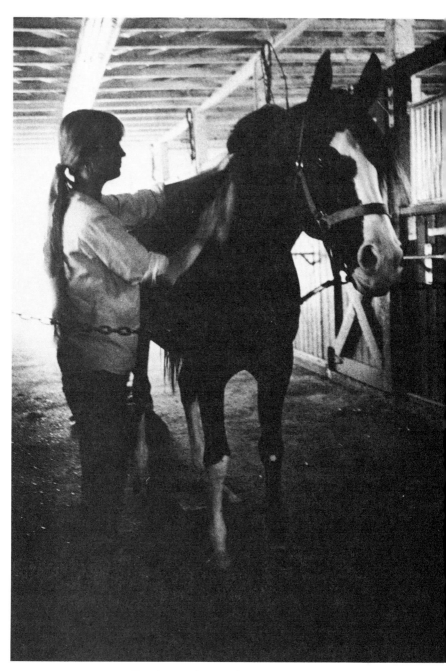

Brush your horse with care every day.

2. Tie your horse when you groom, but don't tie him unless he's been trained to be tied. Even then, be certain to have the lead line tied higher than the horse's withers. A horse can easily break his neck by rearing back against a low-tied shank or cause an accident by getting his foot over it.

3. Train your horse also to be cross-tied, if you decide to use that method while grooming him. Cross-tied or single-tied, it's wise not to leave your horse unattended.

4. Always wear hard boots to protect your feet. Horses don't tread lightly if they step on you.

5. Let your horse know when you're approaching from the rear. Speak up and be sure he responds to your voice. Remember, too, that a horse can kick sideways.

6. When brushing around the horse's hindquarters, run your hand along his back and rest it firmly on the tail, holding it down

and pulling the horse's weight over on the leg closest to you.

7. When picking up either of the horse's hind feet, stand at his side and as close to him as possible. Also, always groom his tail when standing to one side, whether cleaning or braiding it. As always, too, use your voice —make certain he knows you're there.

8. Don't love your horse so much that you're afraid to discipline him. Be gentle and quiet but *firm*.

9. Stallions are often unpredictable. Groom them with caution and respect.

10. Mares "in season" are apt to be un-predictable. And if she has a foal at side, she may be aggressively protective of her off-spring.

11. Proper clipping and trimming re-quire experience, especially around the ears, nostrils, and fetlocks. Use electric clippers

Longe your horse properly—use a loose grip.

but remember that electricity and water don't mix, so move any water buckets a safe distance away. Don't knock yourself out—or your horse! Remember, too, that if a twitch is being used, don't use clippers on his head as he may strike out with his front feet.

12. Keep in mind that your horse needs more than daily good grooming. He needs daily exercise as well. If you're not ready to ride him or don't have the time, the least you can do is to turn him into the paddock or pasture to run and play. Or longe him by working him clockwise and counterclockwise and through all gaits until he's worked up a sweat. It's also a good idea to longe your horse if you've been off him a few days, so he'll be quiet and tractable when you do mount. But make it a policy to work him regularly. A good, healthy, well-fed horse penned up day after day without work can be very difficult to handle.

3
Leading Your Horse

Keep in mind that having your horse at the end of a lead shank is not always the easiest thing in the world. Many accidents can happen when you think you have everything under control and you and your horse are out for a pleasant walk. As lovely as it is, you should be alert and, if possible, never careless. I say "if possible" because I have seen many professional horse people make careless mistakes while their attention was directed elsewhere.

The most "freakish" accident was to the horse of a good friend who was having her horse shod outside the barn while she held the shank. The scene was a beautiful farm, complete with a sparkling pond and a shade tree beneath which the farrier had parked his truck with its portable forge. While the shoe-

Coming back from a pleasant walk.

ing was taking place, she carelessly, and only for a few seconds, let the horse get his head down too low. When he moved his head, he inadvertently struck the farrier's anvil, which caught in his halter. He panicked at the heavy, dangling weight on his head and reared, pulling the shank free of his handler, and going over backward and rolling into the pond. The water was deep, the anvil acted as an anchor, and he drowned.

It was a valuable, beloved horse and his handler will never get over the loss, caused by a single, careless mistake. I'm certain this won't happen to you. But there are a few things I would like you to keep in mind as you go to fetch your horse with lead shank in hand.

* * *

1. If you must get your horse out of a pasture where there are many other horses, take great caution that you don't get caught in a kicking match. This can start if you try to use a bucket of feed to attract your horse. All horses are greedy and want feed all to

themselves, so you may find yourself in the middle of a wild scene!

2. Any lead shank and metal snap to attach it to a halter should be *strong*. Once a horse breaks either, bad habits start. A ¾-inch *cotton* shank with a knot at the end to hold the snap is best. Nylon can slip through your fingers and burn them, as can leather; both are difficult to cut in case of emergency. *Bull snaps* are better than trigger snaps which break easily.

3. Don't ever wrap a lead shank around your hand, arm, or waist. It's far better for you to release a bolting horse than to be dragged. For better control of the horse, use two hands with a knot at the end of the shank.

4. *Never, never* slip your fingers into the halter ring when leading your horse. If he bolts, it may be impossible for you to get them out. A halter ring is intended to hold your lead shank, not your hand.

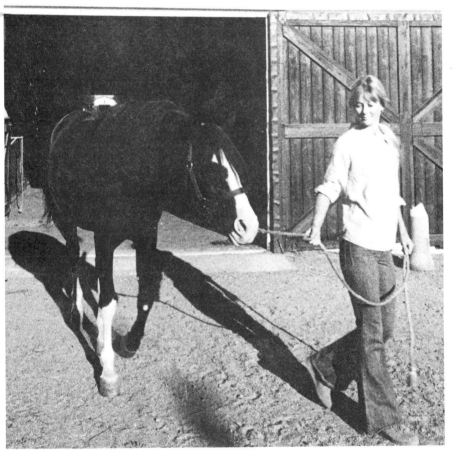

Lead shanks should be strong.

5. When leading your horse, always walk at his left shoulder so he won't run over you. When leading him through openings such as stall doors and gates, be sure they are wide enough and they stay open while you're passing through. Blankets and tack on a horse can easily be caught in narrow openings and startle the horse, causing him to rush through the door or gate and trample the handler.

4
Tacking Your Horse

Your horse will calmly accept the steel in his mouth, the leather weight on his back, and the girth around his barrel, providing the equipment fits properly and does not irritate him in any way. He trusts you to do it right; otherwise you are no friend.

Just as important, however, is your own riding equipment—what you wear on your head, neck, hands, and feet. Before tacking up your horse, check yourself out. Remove any rings or necklaces you're wearing. They can be caught in tack, mane, or tail and you can lose a finger or be choked if for any reason your horse bolts or throws you.

You should be wearing a hard hat if you plan to do any jumping—or, it is my belief, even if you're not jumping. Jockeys and exercise riders wear them all the time, most of them knowing hard hats have saved them serious injury in many a fall. So don't be self-conscious about it or think hard hats are only for "softies."

You should be wearing a shoe or boot with a heel to keep your foot from slipping all the way through the stirrup iron in case of a fall and the possibility of your being dragged with one foot stuck through the stirrup. Wear your sneakers on a tennis court, not riding.

Your horse will accept the steel in his mouth.

With this latter possibility in mind, check your saddle to make certain the safety catch on your stirrup leathers (when riding English) is well oiled and working, so if by any chance you do fall off and your foot is caught in the stirrup iron, the leather will come loose. Better still, ride with the stirrup catches *open*.

Here are a few other rules, many of which you may know but are worth repeating to make certain your horse is tacked properly so you and he can have a comfortable time.

* * *

1. Be certain that the saddle and girth are on securely and that you tighten the girth slowly and in stages. Many horses deliberately expand their lungs when girths are being tightened.

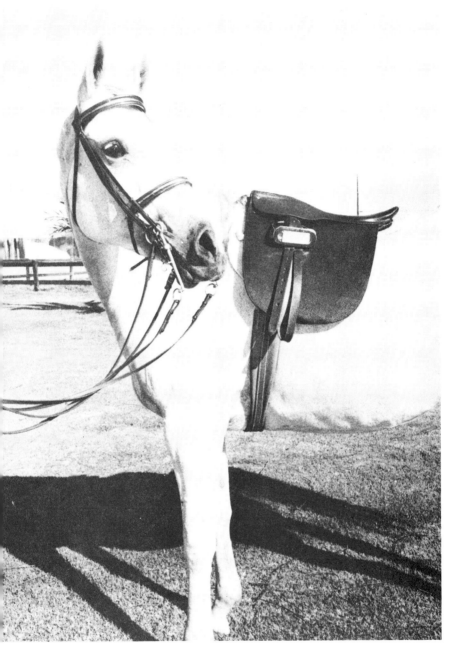

An English saddle.

2. Never use old, worn-out, weak leather for tack. Reins especially wear out by cracking and breaking close to the bit. Girths must often be replaced. Use good quality tack and clean it regularly, for leather dries out and becomes brittle when not taken care of.

3. Be certain your saddle pad lies flat and even under the saddle. And that your saddle fits your horse. Make sure there are no twists in the girth and that it is clean. With the English three-fold leather girth, the open end of the fold should *not* be to the front where the horse's elbow could be pinched in the fold. With a Western stock saddle, many

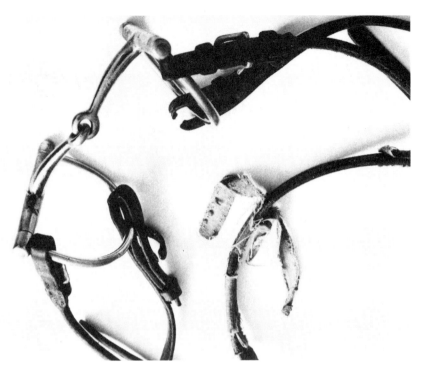

Never let your tack get in this condition.

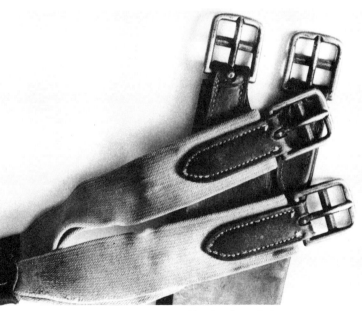

An English leather girth.

accidents have happened because of the back cinch. Unless you are roping a 1,500-pound steer, the cinch should be removed—but, if not, never tightened, and fasten it *after* fastening the front cinch. When you're untacking, unfasten the back cinch *first*. This cinch is not designed to keep the saddle in place and could cause an accident if you're not careful with it.

Western saddle with back cinch (loose).

Ready to be saddled.

Bridling your horse.

Saddled, bridled, and ready to go.

4. Standing martingales must not be tight if you plan to do any jumping.

5. An easy way to bridle a horse, especially one who is inclined to raise his head, is, with the right hand, to take the headstall midway between the top of the bridle and the bit (holding both cheek straps) and your hand resting over the horse's nose with the bit directly in front of his mouth. Your right hand is then free to hold his head while your left hand slides the bit into his mouth.

6. If you're using a curb strap, release one side from the bit before you attempt to put it in his mouth.

Be firm, but do not battle the horse.

5
Riding Your Horse

Now that you are on your horse, you hope he will be willing to do what you ask of him to the best of his ability—at least, that is your goal. Don't try to obtain this by force; do it by being firm, of course, but not by doing battle with him. Leave that kind of action to the hardened professionals who believe that training a horse means his submission to force, which is necessary sometimes. But that is not for you. You have not the strength or experience for it. You are dealing with about a thousand pounds of energy and power to your hundred or so pounds. Your way will be slower and will require more patience, but you'll gain the same end—and the chances are you'll have a better trained horse for it, one who will respond to your commands because he is happy and willing to please you.

Try to achieve unity with your horse.

Remember, to ride a horse is to train him. Every cue to him calls for a response. Responses form habits. Horses learn by habit. This is not only "horse sense" but common sense.

Try to obtain unity between you and your horse. You are not simply a passenger, riding to get something out of him or go somewhere. Try to be a part of him, to have him listen to your mind through your hands and seat which, of course, includes your legs.

It is here, I believe, that the true art in horsemanship is to be found. Your hands, legs and seat work in delicate balance in communicating with his mind. Your goal is to have him "collected" and "on the bit" where he will be most attentive to your commands. You achieve this by pushing him forward with your legs and seat against your

"Close the front door slightly" with your hands.

"still, standing hands," as my old friend and professional horseman Captain Bill Heyer would say. By that he means that you "close the front door slightly" with your hands so your horse is not free to go as he pleases, while your legs and seat push him forward until he meets the quiet but steady resistance of your hands; he then comes together and is "collected," which simply means he is one with you and most sensitive to your commands.

Your hands must not overpower your seat nor your seat overpower your hands.

As I mentioned, this is a delicate balance, for your hands must not overpower your seat nor your seat overpower your hands. The most important thing to remember while you are learning is that *you push your horse together, never pull him together. You must work from back to front, never from front to back.* If you achieve this, your horse will learn quickly what you want him to do, and there is no better feeling than to move with him as *one*.

Out for a pleasant ride.

Here are some other things to keep in mind while riding.

* * *

1. Mounting in and riding through the barn can be extremely dangerous. Your horse could rear, shy, fall. Take him outside and mount there, giving yourself plenty of room. I saw my uncle, a professional trainer and instructor, mount a horse in the barn, contrary to all his warnings to students. The horse reared, causing my uncle to strike his head against a low beam and fall unconscious to the floor. The horse trampled on him in his excitement and my uncle never rode again.

Try to end the lesson on a successful note.

2. Avoid, if possible, any situation that you can't win and the horse can. If your horse gets away with something once, he will be more difficult the next time. So try to end a lesson on a successful note.

3. As in driving a car, don't start moving on your horse unless you can stop. Don't trail-ride until you can control your horse at all gaits and you have learned what he can and will do. Almost any horse will shy at some time or another, so be expecting it and ride with caution on trails.

Watch for unexpected dangers for you and your horse.

4. Try not to ride alone. The "buddy" system is a good one, in case of accidents or problems.

5. Acquaint your horse with cars and trucks, but when riding, keep off roads with heavy traffic. It's a good idea to stay off all roads at dawn, dusk, and night when visibility is poor.

6. When crossing roads on your horse, always cross with others in your group, never separately. Walk your horse; steel-shod feet slip on asphalt or concrete, often causing a fall. Galloping beside the road can be dangerous and trotting can be unsafe and unwise as well; some unforeseen object or dog may cause your horse to shy onto the road. If you ride alongside roads, most state laws require that you ride with the traffic, not against. Check out your state law on this.

Turn your horse to face mechanical hazards on the trail.

7. Be careful not to ride into the back of another horse. If you do, you and your horse may be kicked. Stay at least a horse length behind the horse in front of you. Never leave or approach other riders at a gallop. This can upset their horses as well as your own.

8. If you hear a motor vehicle approaching on a trail from your rear—for example, a motorcycle—turn your horse to face it and stay off to one side of the trail so the driver has a chance to slow down and pass with care.

Your horse is not normally an aggressive animal; his first instinct is flight for self-preservation. Papers blown about, loud noises, anything strange or new will cause alarm. Only through your patience and firmness will he overcome his impulse to flee from whatever frightens him. Therefore, he must learn to trust you, and you must earn his trust through your patience, firmness, and assurance that there is nothing to fear. Regain his attention and make him listen to you.

Watch out for submerged articles in streams.

9. Riding your horse in ponds or muddy water can be dangerous to you and your horse. If you do this, watch out for submerged fence posts, bottles, wire, and other objects. If you're swimming your horse, get off and give him all the freedom he needs to keep his head above water. Horses can swim, but they have their limits, as you have yours.

10. When riding your horse across unfamiliar ground, go at a sensible pace, watching out for holes, wires, and other hazards. Be careful of low tree limbs, especially when you're in a run. Be attentive.

11. When you feel you cannot ride your horse across a stream or through a ditch, dismount and lead him. Be careful to stay out of his path, walking at his left shoulder, when he finally does make a hurried rush or jump to get over or out of obstacles. English stirrups should be run up the leathers so they don't swing against the horse, adding to his excitement.

12. When you dismount to rest or picnic, don't leave your reins hanging to the ground unless your horse is trained to ground-tie. And never bridle-tie your horse—he's apt to break the reins and leave for greener pastures. And the bit can hurt his mouth when he pulls back, cutting his tongue or chipping his teeth.

13. Use a cotton lead rope to tie your horse to a solid object while you're resting. Make a knot that can be quickly released in case of any problems. The rope length should be no more than three feet long so he can't get caught in it, and it should be four to five feet off the ground so he won't get a leg over it. The halter snap should be sturdy so it won't break, if he should try to pull free.

14. An easy walk home is the best way to cool out your horse. Avoid the temptation to gallop him. If you do, he may soon learn to do it in his own way, running out of control in his eagerness to get back to the stable, crossing roads or whatever with little heed to you, his rider.

15. If your horse wants to run away with you, no bit will stop him. The only possibility of stopping him is to attempt to drive him into a large circle, providing you have room. Keep your seat and balance, use both hands on one rein, pulling his head in the direction you want him to go—but not so hard as to throw him off balance and down. Or you might pull hard on one rein and then the other, repeating it often in the hope that your horse will get his mind off running all out and come to a stop.

16. If your horse rears with you and there is a possibility of his going over backward, sit forward, not backward, and don't pull on the reins. You must be forward of his center of gravity to bring him down. Take your feet out of your stirrup irons and be ready to slip off if necessary. But the best way to prevent this from becoming a bad habit is to seek professional help as soon as you're aware of it. A self-rearing horse is a dangerous one.

Walking happily into a trailer.

6
Trailering Your Horse

Loading your horse into a trailer can be a joy or a nightmare. To my mind, nothing is more beautiful to see than a horse walking happily into a trailer after a pat on his hindquarters. Nothing is worse than a horse who refuses and fights being loaded. If the former applies to your horse, you can take him anywhere, to show or to ride new trails. If the latter applies, you'll stay at home, making any excuse possible for not going anywhere when the reason is simply that you do not want to do battle with your horse in order to take him away from familiar surroundings.

It is not only the amateur horse person who may have problems loading a horse. I have seen many professionals who have won ribbons in the ring spend hours of humiliation trying to load their champions and leave the show grounds with some dignity. Sometimes it's the horse's natural, fighting instinct not to enter the confinement of the trailer. But more often it's the fault of the handler. Either way, it's no joy for either horse or owner and both can be hurt seriously in the process.

* * *

Here are some suggestions for dealing with trailer-loading your horse.

* * *

1. Don't buy a horse that already has problems and is hard to load. Check this out before you buy him.

2. Practice loading and unloading your horse at home, using an enclosed area such as a paddock or pasture. Put some kind of bedding from your horse's stall into the trailer so he will feel at home.

3. Make certain your trailer hitch is equal to the weight you're hauling. Double

check to make sure the trailer is hitched to your car or truck securely. Never use a hitch where the ball does not fit perfectly.

4. Avoid sharp fenders, light brackets, and license plates on your trailer while loading your horse so they won't cut him.

5. Check the wood floor in your trailer for any rot or weakness. Also check for rusted spots on metal; they eventually become holes. Old, unsound trailers have caused injury that require the destruction of too many horses whose legs have gone through unsafe floors.

6. Always have a separating partition in your trailer if you're transporting two horses.

7. Be certain the rear doors of your trailer are closed securely, especially if you feel your horse travels better untied.

8. Most horses are tied while being trailered. The best shank to use is a short length of sturdy rubber strap, the kind used to tie

Be certain the rear doors of your trailer are closed securely.

down tarpaulin on a truck carrying open cargo. Place a strong, quick-release snap in a hole at each end of the rubber strap. If the horse tries to pull back, there will be enough give to the strap to keep him from fighting.

9. Never leave grain in the feed box of your trailer to mold and rot. You may later load a hungry horse who eats it and develops colic.

10. Untie your horse and be ready to unload *before* opening the back door. Some horses begin to back out as soon as they know the door is open.

11. When you unload your horse and tie him to the trailer, be certain that he is not able to snag his shank on jutting latches or handles. Close all doors of the trailer so you or your horse won't bump into them.

There is no way to explain the *magic* that some people have with horses.

7

A Personal Opinion

Finally, there is no way to explain the *magic* that some people have with horses. It is almost a mystical gift. It may be that horses sense that these people truly care about them. It may be a handler's sensitivity that accounts for his or her uncannily precise timing and coordination that creates a oneness between horse and rider. Or it may be none of these, but a form of art itself, as creative as any art can be and just as unexplainable and rewarding.

I've learned that one thing is certain. You cannot cultivate this magic, any more than you can any other art form. You have it or you don't have it. But it *is* possible to become a competent horse person without it— as it is for many riders, amateurs and professionals alike. So don't despair. Your goal

Your goal is to have your horse do his best for you because he is happy.

(and mine) is to have your horse do his best for you because he is happy and wants to please you. And that is the best feeling of all.

The scope of this book has been to single out what I consider the most dangerous, the most careless causes of accidents and injuries and to bring them to your attention. Naturally, you should have professional guidance and help when needed. You should also read whatever books are available in your public library on the complete care and stabling, training, and riding of horses. Just as you should join a 4-H or pony club, if one is in your area, and read their manuals.

I hope you will add your own safety rules to the ones I have given you, as well as those rules others may give you. No one is perfect and we all make mistakes, but the fewer we make and the less serious they are, the better.

What I try to do is to make even the most simple rules a habit. For example, I have an old Arabian mare who is my favorite. Her name is Tena (short for Athena, who was the Greek goddess of arts and

Enjoy your horse!

crafts), and while she was very frisky and unpredictable as a young horse, she's too old and tired now to do anything but stand still while being tacked. Nevertheless, when I put on her bridle or take it off, I fasten the halter around her neck and snap on the tied lead shank to the ring. She looks at me as if to say, "This is ridiculous. Where would I be going at my age, anyway?"

Yes, I know it's ridiculous too, but I must work this way because I must remember to do the simplest *safe* things even when they seem unnecessary. If I don't make it a habit, I may not do it with another horse who won't stand still and will break away from me.

And that is what I hope you will try to do: *Make every safety rule a habit.* You might ignore some of them and get away with it time and time again, but there's always the chance that the *next* time you will be hurt. I don't want that to happen to you or to me.

So good, safe riding!

Index